Private View

Jess Edwards

methuen | drama

LONDON • NEW YORK • OXFORD • NEW DELHI • SYDNEY

METHUEN DRAMA

Bloomsbury Publishing Plc, 50 Bedford Square, London, WC1B 3DP, UK
Bloomsbury Publishing Inc, 1359 Broadway, New York, NY 10018, USA
Bloomsbury Publishing Ireland, 29 Earlsfort Terrace, Dublin 2,
D02 AY28, Ireland

BLOOMSBURY, METHUEN DRAMA and the Methuen
Drama logo are trademarks of Bloomsbury Publishing Plc.

First published in Great Britain 2025

A catalogue record for this book is available from the British Library.

A catalog record for this book is available from the Library of Congress.

ISBN: PB: 978-1-3506-0735-4
ePDF: 978-1-3506-0737-8
eBook: 978-1-3506-0738-5

Series: Modern Plays

Typeset by Mark Heslington Ltd, Scarborough, North Yorkshire

For product safety related questions contact
productsafety@bloomsbury.com.

To find out more about our authors and books visit
www.bloomsbury.com and sign up for our newsletters.

The original production of *Private View* premiered in London at Soho Theatre on 2 December 2025, running for 24 performances. Produced by Speakerphone Productions, the cast and creative team were as follows:

Original cast

A	Patricia Allison
B	Stefanie Martini

Original creative team

Writer	Jess Edwards
Director	Annie Kershaw
Set & Costume Designer	Georgia Wilmot
Lighting Designer	Catja Hamilton
Sound Designer & Composer	Josh Anio Grigg
Movement & Intimacy	Ingrid Mackinnon
Casting Director	Jacob Sparrow
Production Management	Production Solutions Group
Costume Supervisor	Carla Anderson-Smith
Stage Manager	Shuyin Stella Wang
Assistant Stage Manager	Lauren Vickers

Producers

Zoe Novello and Sophie Visscher-Lubinizki for Speakerphone Productions.

This is for Jo, Ellen, Jess, Ryan, Theo, Rhian, Max, Noush, Jess, Mads, Ciara, Lenny, Ray and Tia – the people who have picked me up after terrible heartbreak. May we all be there to help mend one another again and again and again.

Private View

Characters

A, *twenty-three years old, female*
B, *thirty-eight years old, female*

A note on the text:

A/B: then a line without words denotes a choice not to speak.

Punctuation is used not necessarily grammatically but rhythmically. Missing punctuation denotes an equivalence of clauses.

A missing full stop denotes interruption (or self-interruption). A new line denotes a change in thought.

Words in square brackets are unspoken. The whole text is to be spoken very fast.

What we denote as 'chance' behavior, in any context, rather than deriving from some ultimately predictable, fully mechanistic behavior of a deterministic physical world, is actually some immense subsumption of a broad distribution of potentialities reflective of all possible resonances and intentions of consciousness with respect to the system or process in question. – Dunne & Jahn, Consciousness and Anomalous Physical Phenomena, 1995

1: Private View

Two people, both alone in the space.

They turn and look, becoming aware of each other for the first time –

An impossibly loud crack and a flash of blinding white light.

A Ohmygod

B What?

A You made me jump

B I haven't seen you before.

A Should you have

B I don't know, you tell me. It's kind of a small world small fucking industry, you know?

A I'm not an artist, if that's what you mean.

B You're obviously the most interesting person here.

A OK

B I can always tell. It's like, a superpower. Find the most interesting person in any room.

A OK. Well – thanks, I guess?

B You've never been to a private view before.

A *shakes her head.*

B The thing you'll learn about private views. They're not glamorous. Everyone pretends they're glamorous. They're boring and tiresome and the white wine is warm and you spend too long standing up.

A Why come then?

B To meet people like you.

A (*smiling*) You don't know me

B   Yet

A *laughs.*

B   What do you think of the work?

A   The art?

B *nods.*

A   Hm. It's all a bit – samey?

B (*loud*)   Hey, someone's got an *opinion*!

A   Shhhh!

B   Let's go and tell the artist he's somewhere over there –

A   No no no no

B   What am I embarrassing you?

A   Yes

B   You have nothing to be embarrassed about. You're luminous.

A   OK. To be honest you're making me feel a bit fucking weird

B   No, I mean it. There's something

Now, they are very close. **B** *reaches out to take* **A**'s *hand.* **A** *is awkward about it – but lets* **B** *touch her.*

An impossibly loud crack and a flash of blinding white light.

2: Romantic

A's *street – busy.*

B   Hey – hey!

A   ?

B   This is insane!

A   Sorry

B   I thought I might never see you again

A   I'm sorry do we

B   It's me. From the private view

A   Sorry

B   That crap exhibition – the other night? No – it was a few weeks ago now. We met

Pause.

A   Oh yeah! Yes. Sorry. Of course.

B   You disappeared. I thought I might never see you again

A   You said that

B   Right!

A   London's a big place

B   I know, right – what are the chances? It's fate.

A   OK

B   (*off her expression*)   Coincidence?

A   There's no such thing as coincidence.

B   Come for a drink with me

A   What?

B   Go on

A   It's – twenty past eleven?

B   Obviously not a drink drink! Just a coffee

A   I can't

B   Why not?

A   I'm busy. I'm on my way to something

B   Sack it off

A   Why should I?

B   Because a coffee with me will be infinitely better than
whatever you're on your way to.
C'mon!

A   No.
I barely know you
Actually, I *don't* know you
I'm not changing my entire day to hang out with you
I don't even know your name

B   Brilliant. Great. Romantic.

A   It's really not.

B   OK

B *turns and walks away.*

A   Hey! Wait –

3: Pints

Outside a pub on the river. **A** *is slightly tipsy.*

A   Wow! Look at the river! You can see so far

B   Ever been to this pub before?

A *shakes her head*

B (*proud*)   It's always quiet. And with that view

A   It's unbelievable.

B   Especially now. At this time – crepuscular

A   What?

B   'Resembling or relating to twilight.'

A (*giggles*)   Show off. Why not say that then

B   Why? Does it sound better

A Maybe

B *Twilight*

A *giggles.*

A moment between them.

A I'm glad we met today

B Me too. Feels so – impossible. Coincidence.

A I told you. There's no such thing as coincidence.

B Feels like you have something to say on this so I think you should go for it.

A (*laughing*)   Fuck off

B No no no please

A OK. Fine. There's this theory. Actually a group of theories. That all these things we think are impossible to explain – coincidence, paranormal activity, even aspects of interpersonal connection – all come down to physics. The fundamental interaction of particles that have been around for millions of years. For forever, really.

B Right. Go on

A A research scientist in Japan did this experiment where he tested the action of consciousness on water – he *thought* at the water – 'I hate you I hate you I hate you I hate you', or 'I love you I love you I love you I love you' and the difference in intention actually changed the molecular bonds in the water

B Fucking hell! That's mad. Kind of. Beautiful.

A Yeah?

B Yeah. How d'you know about all that?

A It's my research specialism. Particle physics and er consciousness. Bit of an outlier.
    People can be sort of weird about it

Beat.

A   I've talked too much haven't I?

B *shakes their head.*

B   You can talk about it with me.

Beat.

A   How long have you been sober then?

B   Hmmmm. Ten years?

A   Woah! Impressive

B   Not really

A   Why?

B   Just took the choice away. Had no choice, had to stop drinking, stopped drinking

A   Did you used to really cane it?

B *looks at them.*

A   Sorry.
Have you done, AA, or anything? Got a mate who did it and swears by it, it's like she's in a cult or something

B   Nahh. I just went cold turkey.

A   Fuck. Hardcore.

B   I guess I am

Beat.

B   Another one?

A   You don't mind?
Being around it I mean?
Buying it for me?

B   Course not. Hardcore, like you said. Anyway, it's been ten years.

If I'm not over it by now I never will be.
Let me. I want to buy you another one.

A (*giggles*)   OK

B *goes to the bar.*

A *waits. Looks at her phone. Drums her fingers*

Suddenly stands, grabs her coat.

Thinks better of it, sits back down

B *is back with a drink for* **A**.

A (*quickly*)   Thanks! Thank you. Hey you never told me
about your work.
What kind of photographs do you take

B   Alright. I used to make these

She gets out her phone.

B   This is kind of what I got famous for

A   Ooooooooooo

B   ?

A   Famous

B   Fuck off

A   You said it

B   *Anyway* – it's people I'm interested in people

A *looks.*

A   It's cool. What's all that light

B   I wanted to catch them at their most vulnerable
So I would create the space the whole sitting
And then just before I took the photograph
I used to set off a firework
So they'd be really

Shocked
I'm interested in that moment of shock

A   OK

B   It's like a special kind of nakedness
I like to strip away the artifice, using the shock
To expose the real person underneath

A   Isn't that kind of – I dunno, violent?

B   Mmmmm
There's a lot of darkness in my work.
And early on when it was coming,
Coming out.
I would panic.
Because I thought, Oh you're bad.
I'm bad.
And then I realised no no I'm not bad. I'm human

Beat.

A   OK

B   Anyway I don't make those any more. I got bored

A   Yeah?

B   Yeah. I got bored with the camera

A   OK

B   And now I make photograms

A   Photograms?

B *shows her on her phone.*

A   Wow

B   There's no camera involved

A   What? How

B   You just have the paper
And then you arrange the subject in the pose

And they have to hold it
Until the photogram develops

A   They're beautiful

B   I wanted it to be like she's in a cage
Made of light

Beat.

B   Come back to mine.

4: Home

B's *flat, the same night.*

A   Fucking hell!

B   What

A   It's just
Huge
All my mates live in rented boxes. This is so
Grown up

B   Hey don't sound so surprised

A   What

B   I am a grown-up

A   Sure
How long have you lived here?

B   Ummmm . . . eighteen years?

A   Yeah? So – you grew up here?

B   No. I bought it when I was like – twenty. No – twenty-one.

A   You're thirty-nine?!

B   Thirty-eight

A   Big difference

B   Hey!

A   When you were twenty-one I was literally five years old

B   You're twenty-three?
Right

A   And you bought this when you were younger than I am now

B   Yeah. It was before Hackney Wick was cool. Everybody thought it was just, like, dog racing and industrial units.

A   Still

B   I never wanted to live somewhere new. Can't stand these new builds, sprouting all over London, all grey, fifty shades of shite.

A   At least a new build is easy to clean

B   Excuse me. This place is clean. It's like –

She points to a patch of floor.

B   Here you can see all the years of paint and footsteps and people living on top of it.
Like – a palimpsest

A   Show off

B   What

A   You love big words

B   Sue me

A   Go on then.

B   Hm?

A   Palimpsest. Tell me what it means.

B   It's a manuscript that has been re-used. A piece of, I guess originally, animal skin, that was valuable, they would write on it once and when they were finished with whatever legal document poem whatever they would

carefully scrape off the writing. And write something
new
But the thing is, you'd always be able to see little traces of
what was left behind, under the new stuff. That's the
palimpsest. The traces left behind.

A OK

B It's actually what I love about London. I feel like you can
see all the traces of all the people and all the things that
they've been feeling left behind. It makes me feel so
alive. When I fly into the city from somewhere else and I
see the whole thing stretched out in front of me – it's
almost intoxicating. Like, I can feel the great vibrating
potential of the city. Of all those lives unfurling, all those
ideas waiting to happen, all those people teetering on
the precipice, the point of no return, about to fall in love
or have sex for the first time or break themselves wide
open

Beat.

B Sorry was that a lot?

A No no

B I feel like I can see them sometimes
The threads of all that human feeling. Gone before. In
the streets. Houses. On bodies. And anyway that's why I
couldn't live in a fucking new build

A It's nice.
It's really nice
I'm jealous

B Well, you can come round
Any time
You're welcome
Whenever you like

They are very close now.

A I don't know what I'm doing here

B   Who cares?

A   I literally just met you

B   I hate it when people use literally as an emphatic

A (*lightly*)   Fuck you

Suddenly, **A** *kisses* **B**.

It surprises **B**.

At first they're both gentle, testing.

Then they kiss each other harder.

It's kamikaze kissing. End of the world kissing.

Another flash of blinding white light and an impossibly loud crack.

5: Please

A corridor in the university where **A** *works.*

A   What the fuck are you doing here

B   Please

A   How did you find me?

B   I went to reception and described you. Turns out there aren't that many people in the Physics department who look like you.

A   Bit stalky?

B   That's not fair.

Beat.

B   How could you just – leave? I woke up and you were gone

A   So?

B   That was like, one of the most romantic things I've ever done. Meet someone, have them slip through my fingers,

bump into them again in the street, spend a whole day
and a night together
You feel it too. I know you do

A I have to get back to work
I'm teaching. There are undergrads in there who
It's hard enough when
People come in looking for the *grown-up*
And then you come in and
This is my, fucking, workplace
OK?

B Come for dinner with me? We could just – talk. Yeah?

A (*suddenly vicious*)   Just fucking leave me alone, OK? You're
being weird

6: Consent

*The street outside **B**'s flat.*

A I'm sorry

B Wow

A What

B I just didn't expect to see you again

A I couldn't stop thinking about you

B Do you want to come in or –?

A Um. OK. Thanks.

They move inside.

A So. I wanted – I needed to come and say sorry.
About freaking out. I do feel it too. You were right

B (*teasing*)   Oh yeah?

Beat.

Say it again

A (*laughing*)   Fuck you! It's just – I've never done this before

B   What the age gap?

A   What no

B   What then

A   I've never been with a woman

B *gets it.*

B   Huh

A   What

B   It just – didn't seem that way. When we were fucking

A *giggles nervously.*

A   OK phew. Didn't want you to think I was some kind of clueless newbie

B   Course not. And. Thank you.

A   For what

B   For trusting me.

Pause.

A *takes a little step towards* **B**.

They kiss. They melt into each other.

A sudden very loud crack and a flash of blinding white light.

A *is draining a glass of wine. A bottle is half empty in front of her.*
B *has something alcohol-free.*

A   Oh my God! I almost forgot
I brought something for us
For this evening

B   Mmm?

A   I thought it could be fun

B   Oh yeah?

A *pulls out a baggie.*

B Christ is that coke

A No obviously not, coke is morally indefensible and more than that it is so over

B (*laughing*)   Right

A It's mandy.

B Right.

A I thought, you know, since you can't drink

B Don't drink

A Right, sure, cos you don't drink
I thought we could take some together
You've done it before, right?

B Course.

A *looks directly at* **B**.

A Do you like it?

B *shrugs.*

A I had some left over from this party
And whenever I take it all I think about is fucking it's like all I want to do is fuck
And when I was at this party – high – all I could think about was you.
And how good it would feel
To do some together.

Beat.

A You're game, right?

Pause.

B Yes. Yeah. Course.

A You OK?

B   What yeah of course I am

A   Don't you want to?

B   Yeah

A   Sure?

B   Of course I'm sure I wouldn't say it if I wasn't sure.
I can handle myself

A *leans in and kisses* **B**. *Teasing.*

A   No one said you couldn't

B   OK.

A   OK. Great. It's – most of a gram.

A *takes out things, starts making bombs.*

B   God.

A   What

B   Just. It's been a while.

A   Reckon it'll be too much for you?

B   Absolutely not.

B *is a bit rattled but covers it.* **A** *is concentrating on the bombs.*

A   So c'mon, tell me

B   Tell you what

A   Where did the money come from? For your flash
bachelor pad

B (*teasing*)   Fuck off

A   'Well that's what it is
I half expected you to have a black leather sofa

B   Hey

A I'm kidding.
      I can't imagine what it must be like to buy a sofa let alone
      a whole fucking flat

B My dad

A Oooh daddy

B Died when I was seventeen

A Fuck. Fuck. Sorry.

B

A I'm really sorry

B It's fine. It was a long time ago

Pause.

B It's not fine actually
      I mean
      It's fine what you said it was a mistake it was a joke
      But I'm not fine about it
      About him
      I actually think about him every day
      D'you know I don't think I've ever told anyone that

A Wow

A *finishes the bombs and hands one to* **B**.

A Cheers

B Ha. Cheers.

A *takes hers.* **B** *doesn't, just holds it.*

B I kind of feel like – it's twenty years twenty-one years
      come on get over it
      Don't want to look
      I don't know, like –
      Weak
      But that's the weird thing about grief – what they don't
      tell you

It doesn't go away
It doesn't even really recede
It just, kind of, changes shape

B *swallows her bomb suddenly.*

A   Thanks for telling me

Flash. Crack.

A ripple in the surface-reality of the evening.

A   I've never known anyone who died

B   Lucky

A   Mmmm. Never even been to a funeral

Pause.

A   I don't really know my dad

B   No?

A   He left when I was very small. Wasn't around. Haven't got any memories of him which is weird because I definitely have memories from that young from that time in my life it's just none of them contain him

B   What happened

A   He fell in love with someone else. I think
I didn't meet him 'til I was nineteen – no – twenty
I've never really spoken to my mum about it

B   What! Are you serious?

A   Mm.

B   I feel like I'm rushing already do you feel anything

A *shakes her head.*

A   Chill it'll creep up on you

B   Are you and your mum close?

A Yeah like super-close
It was just the two of us – for most of my life.
She's incredible actually
We talk about a lot of things. Everything really

B Have you told her about me

A No of course not

B (*laughing*)   Thanks!

A No no. I mean – I told you. It's my first
And also this is like the third time we've met

B Fourth – if you count the private view

A OK

B Go on. About your dad

A Mm.

B If you don't mind

A It's weird talking about him

B Why

A I guess I just – never talk about him
I never feel like I can
But with you it feels – yeah it feels OK it feels like I can

B Good. I'm glad. What's it like now

A What do you mean what is it like
I'm fucking angry with him
He tried to just waltz back into my life and expects to be
Like
A *dad*
Like
A *father*
Or something

B Maybe he's having a go though

A Fuck off you don't know anything about it

Beat.

A   Sorry
Sorry
Sometimes I get so angry about it
Because my mum did so well
So well
She protected me from all of it
I felt like I had a great time as a kid
I *did* have a great time as a kid
Once when I was about twelve I bought something for a
pound
Just a pound
It was something that wasn't going to last
Like some flowers or something like that I don't
remember
And my mum said, why did you buy that
And I said, it's OK it was just a pound
And my mum looked at me and she said,
A pound is a lot of money.
Never think that a pound is not a lot of money.
It is a lot of money.
And then when I was older
I can't remember, sixteen or something
And I think I wanted to do something expensive, I can't
remember what it was
And it wasn't possible
I had my own job by then, waiting tables in this awful
posh awful snobby restaurant
But I didn't have enough for whatever it was I wanted
And I didn't ask her about it.
She told me once that she hadn't bought new underwear
for eight years
I don't actually think she *meant* to say it – it just kind of
came out
She never said stuff like that
It's always stayed with me
And I think it's cos I knew really

That there was no point in behaving
Like a little, bitch, or whatever
Because she protected me from all of it

B   And you think that was cos of him

A   He just *vanished*
And now I've met him I've seen
He's got money. Like, *money.*
Sometimes I think
Would I be a different person?
If he stayed? Growing up with that?
Fuck him.
Fuck him.
He never paid any child support, nothing
Just left

B   That's shit

A   Yeah

Pause.

A   She would say, you only get one dad

B   She's right about that

A   I've worked *fucking hard*
Do you know how many people like me there are doing a
fucking fully funded Physics and Philosophy PhD?
Not many. I worked hard for everything that I've got.
I've *always* worked so hard. Nothing ever wasted,
nothing – I've been so careful – I've taken so much care –
I've worked so hard to make everything *perfect.* Now he's
swooping back in
To try
And take the credit
To come back
And try and be a dad.
It's fucked

Pause.

B   You know
       You probably won't want to hear this but
       I wish I could speak to my dad. Every day.
       Do you ever think you might be able to start again?

A *exhales hard.*

A   It's just
       Hard

B   I know. It's fucking hard. It's probably one of the hardest
       things there is.

Beat.

B   How could he not want to be in your life I'm like – is he
       mad?

A   D'you want to know what scares me probably the most in
       the world?

B   Tell me

A   I'm so scared I'll end up like him

B   Aren't we all scared of that – that we'll end up like them

A   No I mean
       After I met him I was surprised
       We're so alike
       I'm so much more like him than my mum – we have the
       same mannerisms the same ways of speaking all this shit
       you'd think would be learned
       But I'm so scared so scared
       That one day I'll be presented with a choice a big choice
       and there'll be an obvious choice the right choice but I
       won't choose that
       I'll choose the one that is better for me. The selfish
       choice.
       That I'll end up fundamentally selfish

Beat.

A   Don't hate me

B Not possible

A I think I'll probably never have kids because of that

B Wow

A Is this too much? People often tell me I am too much

B No no no no no – absolutely not
I want to know.
I want to know everything about you

A Thanks. For listening to me. It's weird. I feel

B What

A So close to you. Even though we've basically only just met

B *kisses* **A**.

B I feel it too. You know I do

Crack. Flash.

Colours more vivid sensations more intense the world seems sharper, brighter, full of power and energy.

B I sometimes think – it really helps to say it out loud

A What

B The darkest things the things you fear the most to share them

A Yeah?

A *holds out two more bombs.*

A Here

B Thanks.

They both swallow them at the same time.

B (*lightly*)   Have you ever cheated on anyone?

A Why do you ask

B   Guess I was thinking about it when you said your dad met someone else. I wondered – if that was part of the fear?

Pause.

B   I have

A   Really?

B   I'm not proud of it in fact I'm deeply ashamed of it
But I am I have been shall we say a serial infidelitor

A *laughs.*

A   OK

B   I was meant to get married actually

A   Wow really?

B (*lightly*)   That's why I stopped drinking

A   Go on

B   It's a good story actually
It was the night before the wedding
Went out on my own and got completely smashed
Woke up at 5 a.m. somewhere in Soho having had a threesome with two strangers
I remember going into their bathroom
And I had these weird kind of *marks* all over my body

Kind of cuts grazes bruises things
And I didn't know where they came from any of them
And I was looking at my own face in the mirror
And it just didn't look like a face
It felt like it was so easy for something to tear
For the bathroom wall like paper
Or skin
Eyelids
And there was this watery grey light filtering in through the window
And I felt my eyes kind of slide over my face

I was looking at myself and I couldn't quite reconcile that
the face and the self were the same thing
It felt strangely
Disconnected
The only way I can describe it – it's as if my eyes were like
cracked eggs
Uncooked eggs
Thrown against the mirror
And sort of
Sliding down

Beat.

B   The problem with the marks of course was that she
would have seen them and asked where they came from
I mean come on on our wedding night – and of course I
wouldn't have been able to explain. It's fucking hilarious.
That if I hadn't had the marks I probably would have
gone through with it. And I'd still be married to her
now.
Isn't that mental?

Small beat.

B   And anyway. That's when I knew I had to stop drinking

A (*teasing*)   But drugs is OK

B   Apparently so

A   So what happened with the wedding?

B   God. Don't hate me. Please

A   I won't. You can tell me

B   You will

A   Never

B   Alright. I just – didn't go

A   Woahhh

B   It was for the best
She was pissed off
But also I think
Knew that it was a bullet dodged
For both of us
Probably more for her actually

A   Yeah?

B   She wanted kids and I'm not really cut out for that

A   Mmm

B   God.

A   What

B   I can't believe how much we are the same.

A   Errrr

B   The kids thing I mean.

Beat.

B   Anyway
I'm a completely different person now
God I'm rushing

A *giggles.*

B   What

A   Chill! Just let it I dunno wash over you

B   Yes. I know
But what about you? Cheating, I mean

A   I've never really had anything serious
Definitely not *that* serious
But I guess you could occasionally call it cheating yeah
In that I was sort of with the person
And the other person didn't know

B   You know I'll never do that to you, right?

A Cheating?

B Never. Never. I promise.
Hey I was thinking
Do you want to be like, together? Properly?

Pause.

B Say something

A I'm just looking at you.
I really do

B (*like a child*)   YESSS!

A *laughs.*

They kiss.

Crack. Flash.

*Now reality starts to bend – to pulse and vibrate. The space should
feel like it's getting high. The walls, the floor, the soft furnishings
come to life and everything is tactile and fluid.*

They both snort some of the MDMA, perhaps from a key.

B Eurgh

A (*teasing*)   Don't be a pussy!

B I know it's like – a big thing to say. But I've never felt this
way before.

A *laughs.*

B Don't laugh at me

A Bigger than you felt for your almost *wife*

B Well, I think that's probably a good sign if we're honest

A No no it's just – I know
I get it. I feel it too
D'you know entanglement theory?

B What's that

A   Physics again. Everything comes back to physics in the end

B   Go on

A   So it's actually quantum mechanics. My fave. It's basically when two particles interact in such a way that their quantum states cannot be described independently any more

B   Please. You're crediting me with much greater intelligence than I actually have.

A   OK – so like, the two particles collide, and they are so fundamentally altered that they are always linked. So if you affect one – you affect the other

B   Right

A   And do you know what's really wild? Distance doesn't make any difference

B   Go on

A   So the two particles could be miles and miles and miles apart – even lightyears. And if you affect one you still affect the other

B   Wow

A   I know. It really pissed off Einstein actually because he couldn't explain it even though he was involved in its discovery. Know what he called it?

B   What

A   'Spooky action at a distance'

B   (*laughs*)   That's funny. Feels so contemporary.

A   Obvs it's all at a particulate level. Micro of a micro of a micro

B   You're so clever

B *lifts* **A**'*s top.*

A Hey

B *blows a raspberry on* **A**'s *stomach.*

A Woah woah woah stop

B *blows another one.*

A STOP!

A *is slightly hysterical.*

B *blows another one.*

A *screams.*

B *is pinning* **A** *down.*

B Got you

A Please

A *is still laughing.*

B *releases* **A**.

Pause while **A** *recovers her breath.*

A So. Anyway. As I was saying. There is this bit in my research

B Mmmm?

A Basically my research is about the quantum mechanics of consciousness. I'm going to prove that consciousness has many of the same properties as matter. In classical terms – which is all metaphorical really I mean physics in itself is basically a big fucking metaphor to help us wrap our heads around the collective weird shit of the universe But yeah in classical terms if they've considered consciousness at all it's as a particle – like, localised, in space and time, capable of only, smashing into a few things nearby

B Right

A   But it could also be like waves. It could be *both* wave-like and particulate in nature

B   Mmmhmmmm

A   OK so think about light, yeah? Put it in some circumstances, light behaves like discrete particles. But it can also, like *become* a wave when it needs to
And everyone thinks science – especially physics – is like objective or whatever like a real hard fact but there's no such thing. We've conceived all of this via our consciousness. It's the classic 'hard problem'. We've like – made it all up. By observing, yeah, but still. Consciousness is necessary in observation – relativity, right? If you're observing something, simply by the fact of your observation, you change it.

B *laughs.*

A   What

B   This is such a fucking conversation for high people –

A   Fuck off! You know exactly what I mean anyway

B   Oh yeah?

A   Your photograms.

B   Mmmmmmmmmmmmm?

A   The observer – in this case, *you* – changes things. Changes the subject into an object

B   Ha. You're right. Keep going. I like it. I like listening to you.

A   OK. Consciousness has basically invented particles and waves. And sometimes when it perceives stuff around it, finds it necessary to alternate between the two – with light, yeah? So, why would consciousness not also find it useful to represent itself in this way? As both waves and particles?

B   And so what

A   If consciousness is wave-like. It's not just localised – smashing into stuff. It *can*. It can change the world. And like entanglement – distance wouldn't make any difference.

B   Woahhhh

A   They've done a bunch of experiments with um basically like random number generators? And the operators attempt to change the results using just their intention. And it does. It works.

B   Fuck.

A   Yeah

B   So everything is intention?

A   I guess that's one way of putting it.

B   Fuck. That's – a lot of power.

A   I guess it is. The power to change the world.

Crack. Flash.

Later. Darker. Hotter. Sweatier.

A *and* **B** *have been fucking. They have taken all of the mandy. There is a wildness and sensuality to how they touch each other, speak to each other. Music plays. They dance together. They are all over each other.*

A   Oh my GOD I love this song!

B   I'm obsessed with you

A   What?

They dance – as the song ends –

B   You are so fucking hot

A   Shut up

B   And. You're so clever

A   Ha. Thanks.

B   You're such a clever girl.

A   Mmmmmmmm

B   But you're so inexperienced

A *looks up at* **B**.

A   You're right. I am

B *brushes her hand down* **A**'s *body.*

B   Sometimes I wonder if you really know what's good for
you

A *shudders involuntarily.*

B   Or if you need to be taught a lesson.

Their eyes are locked together.

B   Want me to keep going?

A   Keep going

B   It's like
A game
You know?

A   I want you to keep going

B *runs her hand down* **A**'s *body, slowly, deliberately, teasing.*

B *gently grazes* **A**'s *crotch with her fingers.*

A *(very quiet)*   Please

B *holds them there in suspended animation for a moment.*

B   There's something I have to ask you

A   Now?

B   You are OK about the age gap right?

Pause.

A Honestly?

B Always

A It feels like it's not there I feel like we're the same

B Yessssss

B *touches* **A** *again.*

A *is breathing hard.*

A (*very quiet*)   Fuck

B It's you. You're an old soul. I feel like there's no space
between us

A *breathes harder.*

A I need. I'm
Please

B How much do you want it

A So much
Please

B I want to see how much
I want you to beg

A Oh God
Please
I want it so much
I need it
I need it
I need it
Please

A *takes hold of* **B**'s *hand and presses it to her.*

B *whips her hand away.*

B You're not allowed to, until I say
You wait. Until I say

A (*very quiet*)   Oh my God

B *kisses* **A**. *Deep. Hard.*

B   Now

A *cries out.*

They break apart.

A   Do people know that sex can be like this? How does
anyone ever get anything *done*?

B *laughs.*

A   I feel like there's pure fucking light fucking energy
flowing through my veins like this golden light bursting
out of me.
You have changed me. You have. Fundamentally altered
the fabric of my existence.

B   I feel so lucky. To be your first.
You're everything. You're sexy. You're so clever. You're
all the things. How can you possibly be all the things?

A *kisses* **B**. *Hard. Deep.*

B   Wait. I have the *best* idea

A   What

B   Your lab

A   What?!

B   Is it open?

A   Uh, yeah it's twenty-four hours but

B   Let's go!

A   BUT it's controlled conditions I'm obviously not allowed
to bring just any motherfucker in

B   I want to see your work. I want to see you, really see you

A   No no no

B Don't you trust me

A Of course I do

B We'll be careful

A (*giggling*)   OK

B C'mon

7: Experiment

The same night. A's lab. They are both still high and giggly with it. The world seems blurry, euphoric. A fiddles with a screen.

A Shhhhhh!!

B *giggles*

A We have to be quiet –

B Wow

A Thanks

B What *is* it?

A It generates a metric for intention. Tries to. In real time.

B What!?

A Like I was saying – other researchers, they've only tried it with the random number generator? And the operator's intention affected the result?

B Yeah

A This is much more sophisticated. Look –

She closes her eyes for a second, concentrating.

Light plays across the screen.

B Wow
It's beautiful

A Thanks

B   You built this?

A   Yeah.

B   Wow
You're so
Clever

A *squirms.*

B   Can I try?

A   OK – but – it doesn't work with everyone straight away –
can take a bit of practice

B   Yeah yeah let's have a go

She stands where **A** *stood, faces the screen, closes her eyes.*

Nothing happens.

A   Just – *relax*
Try to sort of – let it creep up on you

B *does.*

A *goes and touches* **B**.

An explosion of light across the screen.

B *opens her eyes.*

B   Christ. It's so beautiful. I can't believe you made this

Light plays over the screen.

B   Fucking hell. It's so –
It reminds me

A   Of your photograms

B   Yeah

Beat.

A   You're right. We are the same

They watch the light together for a moment.

A   We know so little about the brain. So little. It's all so new. 1.1 trillion cells. 100 billion neurones. And within each one – 5000 synapses connecting it to other neurones. It has to be physics. The numbers are too big. The things are too small. It's a micro of a micro of a micro. And consciousness – our uniquely human attribute, as far as we know

A stab of light.

A   What was that one?

B   I was thinking of

A   The first time we met?

B *nods.*

B   It's so beautiful. Did you design it deliberately to be this beautiful

A   We have this theory. About compound intention
When you take bonded pairs and their intentionality works together
It's like – it seems like it can be – extremely powerful. Two consciousnesses interacting.

B   Wait

B *takes out her phone.*

A   What

B *puts on a song.*

B   Oh my God I love this song

A *giggles.*

B   I want you to dance

A *bursts out laughing.*

A   What no this is my *lab.*

A *is still laughing, high.*

B   C'mon

They start to dance together, the machine still on behind them.

They start apart then get closer. It's hot. They are both aroused. Maybe it gets closer to fucking than dancing.

A   What are you thinking of

B   You, your body
How incandescent you are

A   The way you look when you

B   The way your whole body shudders when you'r
about to
How different you are since we met

A   How gentle you are inside that no one sees

B   How I have unlocked you

The light play on the screen explodes.

The sound of a door slamming shut. **A** *springs back from* **B** *as if she's been burned.*

A   Fuck!

B   What was that oh God

A   We need get out of here

B *giggles.*

A   Fucking, go!

8: Safe

Mid-morning, next day. The light is bright and knife-sharp.

A   FUCK

B   What

A   I'm fucked

B   What are you talking about

A   That security guard. He saw us and reported it. They
think someone broke in and now there's a fucking
investigation and this morning, my department director
decided to shut down the whole site

B   OK, let's just take a deep breath here

A   Fuck off!

B   OK

A   We're all working with quantum technology you fucking
idiot! It's extremely sensitive!
Everyone is having their data systems audited, their
physical experiments halted

B   This all sounds like a bit of an overreaction –

A   Some people are doing fucking MOD research in that
place! I am such an idiot. I can't believe I let you talk me
into this.

B   OK

A   Obviously they know who was in there. There was
basically no one onsite because it was the middle of the
fucking night. And when they look back at the CCTV
what are they going to find? Oh right yeah it's me
tapping in followed by someone who tailgates?! YOU.
They've called a Research Integrity Panel. I might lose
my fucking job. Because of you.

B   I'm sorry

A   Oh you're sorry! OK, great, brilliant!
Do you have any idea how serious this is?

B   It's going to be OK. I'm going to make this OK. We can
find a way through this

A *throws something. It smashes.*

B   Right

A   We CAN'T. You don't get it. You don't. You live a life of unfathomable privilege. You think work is when you get your pictures on a fucking billboard and you barely lift a finger. You have no concept that anything you do would make any difference to anything or have any impact on the world which is why you talked me into breaking into my own fucking lab and sabotaging my whole career everything I've worked so hard for I was so careful I care so much and now it's FUCKED. Because of YOU.

Pause.

B   OK. You do not mean that. You're upset

A   Fuck you don't tell me what I feel

B   *(calm)*   You're upset, and we're going to get through this together

Pause.

B   Come here

A *crumples into her arms.*

A *cries.* **B** *strokes* **A**.

B   There. We're going to make it alright. Together

A   I'm just sick
Of being the youngest in the department
Sick of being the joke one. Token

B   You're not

A   You don't know that

B   Let's make a plan. What do you need to do

A *takes a deep shuddering breath.*

A   If they only declare it compromised. That's if they don't find out it was me and put me on probation. I'll need to repeat the whole experiment. Get new results. Clean ones. In about a quarter of the time. It's basically

impossible
I've got my next leg of funding riding on this piece of research.
And they already think I'm not heavyweight – that what I'm doing is like woo woo bullshit, not really quantum mechanics.
I've got to submit in the next few weeks.
And if I don't make it work – that's it. My career is over. There's no way I can afford to continue without the funding. I didn't want to tell you. I felt

B   Oh no don't say that

A   This is me. This is all of me. I am this work I can't separate it from me and so if I lose it then there's no more me that's all there is I cease to exist

B   I know. I really do know. I feel like that too. About my work. My photograms. It *is* me.
And I forgive you by the way

A   For what

B   What you said before. About my work.

A   It's weird

B   What

A   Sometimes before – other people I've been with. They've been all like, 'you love work more than you love me'. It's totally different. I don't fuck work. But I feel like with you – you get it. You understand.

B   I do. I really do.

A   We are the same.

B   And – it looks like I might get a new solo show soon. It'll be a shit-tonne of work. So you see? We can be in this together. Yeah?

A   OK

B   Pose for me

A   I can't I'm not going to have time

B   Come on! It'll be amazing. Once you've got the experiment done. And I'll help you I'll cook for you I'll look after you I'll take care of you. And then when it's done – pose for me. Yeah?

A   OK. Yeah

B   Promise?

A   Yeah

B (*like a child*)   YESSSS!
          Here. You need me to look after you

*She wraps **A** in a blanket. Holds her. Strokes her. **A**'s body finally relaxes.*

A   This sounds intense but I feel like we're going to be together forever

B   What would you do if I died?

A   Fuck. Don't
       I feel
       You complete me

Pause.

B   I

A   You can

B   You know what I'm thinking don't you

A *nods.*

A   It's OK. You can say it now

B   OK?

A   OK.

B   I love you.

A very loud crack and a flash of blinding light.

9: Youth

Outside, a public place, night.

They are both a little breathless

A   Oh my God!

B (*smiling*)   What?

A   Don't give me that

B (*smiling*)   What?

A   That was so fucking hot

Beat.

A   Stop pretending you do this kind of thing all the time

B   Well –

A   Come on

B   Right. You've got me.

A   So. Fucking. Hot.

Beat.

A   I've never done that before?

B   Which part

A   Shut *up*! In a toilet in a restaurant toilet obviously

Have you?

B   No no no I have
But never before
In public
Have I come so hard

A   Shhhhhh!

B   What

A   Someone will hear

B   So what?

A   Oh my God

B   You love it

Pause.

A   I've been thinking

B   ?

A   You always

B   What

A   You always pay for me

B   So?

A   It feels. I dunno. Unfair?

B   Well. I'm – what was it you said? – a capitalist wanker who thinks naked girls on Old Street roundabout is art? And I've had many, many more years on you to acquire my vile capital. What if I deserve to redress the balance?

A (*laughing*)   OK

B   What could possibly be unfair about that?

A   Are you sure

B   Of course I'm sure

A   Alright.

B   I love it. I love buying you dinner.

A   Thank you.

Pause.

A   I can't stop thinking about how hard you came

B   Mmmmmmmm

A   You know there is one thing that I do have
That you don't

B   What d'you mean
There are loads of things you have I don't
An incredible sharp scientific inquiring mind for one
thing
A proper job
For another

A   I see you looking at me sometimes
In the morning especially
I know you feel it too

B

A   You're jealous

A *starts to press* **B** *up against a wall.*

B *is surprised. But they're into it.*

A   Don't say anything

B *nods.*

A *touches* **B***.*

A   I see it in you
When we wake up together
And you look at me
At my body
At the tautness of my skin
And underneath the muscles the bone
I can feel it radiating off you it's like a white white heat
You're so jealous
Of this thing I have
That you don't
That you can never
Never
Never
Get back

They are very close. Both breathing hard.

A   Because deep down you know
That cos I am young
And you are not
And I've got this chance to do whatever I want with my life
That you'll never get back
And you can't bear it
And you feel like somehow being near me being with me
Some of it some of my aliveness will seep into you
Give it back to you
But it never will

A *gets her hands around* **B**'s *throat.*

B *takes a deep shuddering breath.*

A   And that kills you
Doesn't it. Doesn't it. Doesn't it

Both breathe hard. Their breathing intensifies.

A   I'm right aren't I

B *cries out.*

A sudden loud crack and a flash of blinding white light.

10: Together

B's *flat, early.*

B   Don't go. Please. I never want you to leave.

A   I have to

B   No you don't. Just stay

A   It's not up to me is it?

B   Pretend you're ill. Stay here in bed. With me

A   Obviously I can't do that. Not all of us have schedules that – I have to make sure the lab

B Yeah yeah yeah – you're so busy and important

A Shut up

B Hey! Shall we move in together

A What

B We spend all our time together anyway. Seems silly. Paying two sets of council tax. Electrics. Seems silly?

A

B What

A It's just

B What?

A I obviously can't afford to live somewhere like this

B Don't be silly

A Don't call me that

B No no no no no not like that I just mean that doesn't matter

A What do you mean

B I mean I'd cover it

A Seriously?

B Yeah. Course. I paid off the mortgage like . . . five years ago?

A Wow

B And it'd be weird me taking your money I mean what would that make me, your landlord? That would be

A So weird. Yeah.

B Great. That's settled then

A I could cover the bills?

B Seriously, don't worry about it. I earn, what – literally six times what you earn?

A Literally?

B It's not an emphatic it's maths. And anyway. Think of it like – a donation. My contribution to the furthering of science?

A A donation? What does that make you my fucking patron?

B No it makes me your *partner*. Jesus. I was kidding. But seriously – it's fine. I pay them anyway. It makes no difference to me. I want you to feel like it's yours.

A I guess we do spend all our time together anyway. Yes.

B Yes OK like yes?

A Yes let's do it!

B YES
What did I do. What was I doing with my life. Before you?

11: Softly

B*'s flat.*

B You know you can bring your stuff
You're like a ghost
Barely there

A Hmmm?

B I mean you've moved in properly now. Your stuff

A This is my stuff

B *laughs.*

A What

B What like one bag and a box of books?

A   Yes

B   That cannot be all your stuff what about furniture

Beat.

B   I'm really happy to make room I want this place to feel
       like yours too, you know

A   I don't have any furniture
       I don't have any other stuff
       This is my stuff

B   OK

Pause.

B   You tread lightly

A   I do

B   Softly

A   What

B *recites from memory.*

B   Had I the heaven's embroidered cloths
       Enwrought with golden and silver light
       The blue and the dim and the dark-cloths
       Of night and light and the half light
       I would spread the cloths under your feet:
       But I, being poor –

A *sniggers.* **B** *gives her a little shove, playful.*

B (*louder*)   But I being poor have only my dreams.

Pause.

B   I have spread my dreams under your feet

Pause.

B   Tread softly. Because you tread on my dreams.

Pause.

A   Nice

B   Yeats

A   Impressive

B   Thank you. Romantic?

A   You are ridiculous

B   Hey

A   Anyway I don't need nice stuff do I
You are the queen of stuff
The queen of luxy shit
I don't need anything I've got you

12: Private

B's *flat.* **B** *is on her phone.*

B (*at phone*)   Fuck's sake.

A *comes in from outside in a coat.*

B (*smiling*)   Hey gorgeous
Just one second

A *stands, hovers.*

B (*at phone*)   Cunting wanking tossing bastard

A   Errr

B   Just a second!

A   Should I . . .?

B   No no no no no no

Beat.

B (*at phone*)   Fine! Have it your way!

She locks the phone and pockets it.

B   There!

Kisses **A**.

B   You have my undivided attention

A *laughs.*

A   Finally

B   Sorry

A   I stopped on the way home

B   Do you want a glass of wine?

A   I got something for you

B   Oh yeah? Wine?

A   Sure. Thanks.

*A pause where **A** waits for **B** to pour. A glass of wine for **A** and something alcohol-free for **B**.*

A   I wanted to surprise you

She opens the coat to show something she's wearing underneath.

B *stops with the drinks.*

*A moment where **B** is speechless, then.*

B   Wow

A   Yeah?

B   Yes

A   Thanks

Beat.

A   I've never dressed up for anyone before
I liked it
The feeling of walking through London
Wearing this – for you – and it being secret, private
People looking at me and not knowing

A *gets closer to* **B**.

A   It's you I
I want
To please you

A *gets even closer but they are not touching.*

B *hands* **A** *the glass of wine.*

B   You absolutely have succeeded
Well done

A *drinks.*

She never takes her eyes off **B**.

B (*testing*)   Good girl

A *shivers.*

B (*testing*)   Take the coat off

A *does.*

B (*more sure of herself*)   Go and stand over there

A *does.*

B   I want to see you

A   Here?

B   Don't say anything
Don't speak
Unless you are spoken to
OK?

A *nods.*

B   Unless I tell you

Their eyes are locked on each other.

A spell being cast between them.

B   Don't do a single thing
Unless I tell you

A *nods.*

B   You don't get to choose
I get to choose
And you do exactly as I say

A *shudders.*

B   Do you understand?

A *nods.*

B   I said, do you understand

A   Yes

B   You can have a drink.

A *takes a sip of wine.*

B   More

A *drinks more.*

B   Good girl.
Put the glass down

A *does.*

B   Now
Turn around
I want to look at you
I want to know that you're mine
I want to know every part of you
No don't come any closer
There
Turn around
Fucking hell, your body.
You're mine. You're mine. I want –

A   I need you to touch me

B (*very quiet*)   Silence.

A *is silent.*

B   Do you like that?
You're allowed speak.

A   Yes

B   Do you like me looking at you

A   Yes

B   What do you want

A   Whatever you want. Anything. Anything

B   Bend over. From the waist
I want to see how you look

A *does it.*

A   Please. I want you to touch me

B   Did I say that you could speak?

A *shakes her head.*

B   We can't have that

B *gets out her phone.*

The spell is broken.

A   What

B   What?

A   What the fuck why would you get your phone

A *covers herself with the coat.*

B   What! I was just going to take a picture you look so fucking hot –

A   As a punishment?

B   What

A   You were going to take a picture of me like this as a punishment?

B   What no

A   You were
I don't like that

I don't
This is private?
OK?

B Of course it is of course it's private
I completely respect that
That was never my intention
Imagine
It's me too
It's like
A game. Our game.

A *nods.*

B Totally private

A Good

B Christ. Imagine if someone heard me talking to you like that my God I'd be instantly cancelled

A You have done so many cancellable things I'm amazed you've escaped for this long

B Hey!

A Well, you have

B Hopefully the good people of the future will be able to separate the art from the artist and even after I am consigned to the scrapheap of internet cancellation my profound body of work will prevail

A You are ridiculous

B That's why you love me

They kiss.

A I liked it

B Oh yeah?

A You talking to me like that. I really liked it.

B I liked it too.

A blinding flash of white light and an impossibly loud crack.

A *and* **B** *kissing, incredibly deep.*

A blinding flash of white light and an impossibly loud crack.

B *holds* **A** *in front of them, violent but sexual.*

A blinding flash of white light and an impossibly loud crack.

A *is doubled over in pain as* **B** *leaps back.*

B   Sorry sorry fuck sorry

A   Ow!

B   Christ! Are you OK?

A   Oooft. Yes. Yeah. I'm fine – I think

B   Show me

A *does.*

B   Oh darling. You're bleeding. I'm so sorry. Here, let
        me –

She goes to get things to clean up.

A   I don't mind

B   What

A   I wanted it

B   Yeah?

A   I want you
        I want you
        To ruin me

13: Work

B's *flat.* **A** *is working on a laptop.*

Silence. **B** *watches* **A**. *Then –*

B   There's this gallery interested

A   OK

B   It's the Mayfair one

A   Cool

B   They've got spots in the Bowery and in Dubai as well so
yeah so I'm delighted really that they're even interested
but they haven't made a decision yet and they usually do
like dead artists always actually so it's a long shot.
Unless they already think I am a dead artist

A   Great

B   Are you even listening to me?

A   What?

B   I'm trying to tell you about this this very big deal for me
this Mayfair gallery this gallery of my dreams and you're
not even stopping what you're doing

A *closes the laptop.*

B   Thank you

A   You could have waited 'til I'd finished

B   Oh come on, I've been waiting all day to tell you

A   Sorry

B   I'm excited, you're my girlfriend

A   Sorry

B   All I want to do when I get a piece of news like this is
celebrate it with you

A   OK yes sorry

Beat.

A   What

B   You just don't look very pleased that's all

A   Fuck's sake

B   What

A   I was in the middle of something!

B   You're always in the middle of something

A   Oh, grow up

B   Excuse me?!

A   You don't have to compete for my attention we can both be adults here

B   Adults. Right.

A   ?

B   Which one of us pays for this place

A   Woah

B   Which one of us actually pays for everything

A   God

B   Maybe take a look at that and ask yourself which of us is the *adult* here

A   What is this?

Silence.

A   What is going on here?
I checked with you I checked you said it was fine you said you didn't mind
About paying for things
Sometimes

B *gives a derisive laugh.*

A   You know I have to make my funding and my teaching stipend go quite far you know that. I thought you liked it. Paying for things. You said you liked it.

B *says nothing.*

A   Look. It's not my fault the world totally devalues the kind of academic inquiry that I'm doing while they put what you do on some kind of pedestal

B   What's that supposed to mean

A   Nothing

B   No come on, 'let's both be adults here'

A   No

B (*loud*)   Come on

A   Fine – I find it astonishing that the world puts this value this abundant value on what you do but deems my work to be, from a financial perspective, pretty much worthless. You know if you work it out by the hour I basically get paid minimum wage? But I am supposed to be happy, to be grateful, to be so proud that my work has been recognised in this way that I get to be even trying even attempting to submit a PhD on the subject which is such a fucking outlier that few funding bodies will touch it with a barge pole and even more, especially as a woman, as a person, as a young person as someone who looks like me.
I should be grateful. Because I get to be so special
And because I'm so good. But you know what? You can't eat praise.

B   Right. OK. So where does that leave me then?

A   What do you mean

B   My work is meaningless?

A   I didn't say that

B   'Pedestal'? Was the word you used, I believe

A   Yes but

B   Do you know how fucking hard I worked to have even a chance of that pedestal?

A   OK but you did also have

B   And how long the phrase '*enfant terrible*' has followed me
around? I think it's even in this fucking marketing copy

A   Oh shit, someone wrote the wrong fucking thing about
you in some marketing copy but you're still getting paid
five figures for one piece of work boo fucking hoo
Seriously. Listen to yourself. It's pathetic

B   So. All I'm good for is supporting your career then?
Subsidising you and paying for nice stuff for you and I
don't know being your fucking patron until you can get
the scientific world to understand your poor
unrecognised genius?

Pause.

B   If that's the way you feel then maybe you should just go

A   What
No. Come on. No. That isn't what I meant

B   What did you mean then

A   I'm sorry
I'm sorry
I love you. I'm sorry

B   Let's do the shoot

A   What

B   I want to do the shoot

A   Now?

B   Now

14: Shoot

*Outside. Night. Very dark. In fact, complete darkness apart from
when* **B** *uses her lighting equipment. Most of the conversation we
hear, rather than see.*

A I thought you never got complete darkness in London

B Well, you've never been to the heath at night before

A Can you see me
I can't see anything

B Just give it time your eyes will adjust

A flash of blinding white light which illuminates them for a second.

A Fuck!

B Sorry

A Warn me next time

B Sorry I'll try
Just trying to get it right

The sound of **B** *spreading paper or something on the rough ground.*

A Aren't you afraid of someone coming

B What
No
I've done this dozens of times

A But are they always [naked]

B Of course that's the only way you can get the definition
of form get the shape on the paper right

A I didn't realise

B What?

A You never said

B You've seen my work I assumed you knew

A And it's always at night

B Yeah of course that's the only way this process works
This process I invented
My process

A Right yeah
Sure

B What

A What

B I can hear you
Being weird

A I'm not being weird I think it's actually totally normal
To feel a bit I dunno strange
About your partner spending all this time with beautiful
thin beautiful naked women

B Right

A What

B What about your research partner?

A WHAT?

B Exactly

A What d'you mean

B I feel about them like you feel about your research
partner

She adjusts something in the mechanism.

B It's nothing
It's work

She makes one final adjustment.

B Ready

A OK

B So?

A OK

B Take off your clothes

A *starts to undress.*

B Slower

A OK

B (*very quiet*)   Fuck
                        Look at you

A Can you even see me

B I can see you
       I see you

A OK

B Keep going
       Fucking hell
       Your body

B *shudders.*

A *goes even slower.*

FLASH.

A Fucking Jesus –

B Sorry I'll remember to warn you next time
       Right
       Here

She arranges **A** *in the pose on the paper on the floor.*

A Ow

B It's OK just relax into it

A I don't think my body actually goes that way

B Try
       Please

A *gasps.*

B Perfect

FLASH.

A Ow

FLASH.

A   Please

FLASH.

A   It's hurting

FLASH.

B   God. Just try.

Pause.

A   OK

B   OK

B   I love you

A   I love you

B   I know

15: Celebrate

B*'s flat, late at night.* **B** *is hiding.*

A   Hello? Hello? Oh fuck! I couldn't find you anywhere.

B   I've been waiting for you.

A   Here?!

B   I didn't know where you were.

A   Come on, that's not true

B   Are you calling me a liar?

A   Come out from under there.

B   Stop treating me, you're treating me, like a fucking child

A   Hey, this is ridiculous

B   Don't call me that!

A Hey, I've got something to tell you. The funding. The next stage of my funding. I got it. I feel like I dunno like I'm saved! And tonight – I thought – we could celebrate?

B OK

A OK? What the fuck's that supposed to mean? Aren't you happy for me?

B Well, I guess that's it then.

A What

B You don't need me any more.

A What are you talking about

B You've got it, this thing, this big thing. And now you don't need me. Any more. You'll move on with your life. That's it.

A This is – I thought you would be happy for me?

B Oh yeah I am

A You don't look it

B How can I be when it's this or me? You're only with me cos you need me to pay for things

A You know that's not true. This is insane

B Fuck you don't call me that

A OK

B You do love it. You do love your work. More than you love me. It makes me – it makes me want to hurt myself.

Pause.

B I'm going

A WHAT?

B This is this is it it's us we're done I'm going

A   Right. OK. Even though this is what I want most in the world – apart from you this us.

B   I'm just trying to tell you how I feel –

A   What do you want from me?

Pause.

A   If it's what you want. I'll turn it down. I will refuse it.

B   God. No no no no no no no

A   What?

B   I'm sorry. You're right. You're right! This *is* insane. I want this – for you, I want this and I am happy I am happy I am!

A   OK

B   I am

A   OK! Great. I'm glad

B   Lovely

A   Lovely

Pause.

B   Look. I came back and you weren't here. And – it's actually happening. My exhibition.
Mayfair. The one I wanted. The one I never dreamed would actually happen. You know?

A   What? That's amazing!

B   I know. And I just – I really wanted to tell you and you weren't here. I'm not a failure

A   No one ever said you were a failure

B   I'm not, a FUCKING FAILURE

A   You're not you're not of course you're not. You're a genius

B   I sometimes feel like I am the negative image of you. Like what I do only makes sense in light of you. And sometimes it makes me feel

A   What

B   Without you? Do I exist

A   OK

B   Like, if you're not touching me does my body even exist any more

They hold each other.

A different kind of hold.

16: Us

B's *flat. Early evening.*

B   What about this?

A   Immaculate. It's perfect.

B   You said that about the other one

A   It's you – you're perfect.

B   Hmm I dunno about that
How does it take you like three minutes to get dressed
You look good in everything

A   Hardly

B   You do you put things on and you look so gorgeous and lean and –

A (*pointed*)   Young?

B   Alright young! Makes me feel about 105 years old

A   Shut up you look great

B   The only trouble is you look so good in everything I just want to take it off –

B *pushes* **A** *lightly down, flirting.*

A   I don't know if we have time

B *starts to tickle* **A***.*

A   Hey no no no no

B *tickles* **A** *harder.*

A   Argh! Stop stop

She is hysterical.

Laugh crying.

A   Please no no

She is pinning her down.

A   I'm literally – I'm going to die

B   Got you.

Finally she releases her.

A   Listen

B   What's the matter you're being weird

A   I'm worried about the picture.

B   What do you mean

A   I think we should take it out.

B   WHAT

A   I don't want it to be in there. It's private.

B   What are you talking about

A   I just don't know if I want people to see to know in that way

B   People already know.

A   It's like

B   What

A   It's like the way we sometimes talk you talk to me
which is which should be
It's private
Just between us
You know?

B   It's out there. If we take it out now people will think

A   Doesn't it matter what I think?

B   People will think you're ashamed of me

A   That is absolutely not what this is about
God
I regret it. OK? I regret us taking it

Pause.

A   I wish it didn't exist

B   You do not mean that

A   It is private.

B   No. No. That picture – it's us. It stays.

Pause.

A   You were right. About the other one. You should change.

17: Secret

A toilet cubicle in a gallery in Mayfair. Both of them are breathing hard.

A   Fuck
Fuck
Fuck
That was sensational
That was so fucking hot
You're amazing
God you look

B claps her hand over A's mouth.

B   Shut up

A   ?

B   I don't want anyone to hear us

Slowly takes her hand away from **A**'s *mouth and caresses her face.*

A *is still breathing hard.*

They kiss.

B   Look at your beautiful throat

B *kisses* **A** *there.*

B   You're so
You're
Perfect

A   Thanks. Thank you

Pause.

B (*lightly*)   I saw you, by the way

A   ?

B   Talking to her

A   Who

B   That's enough

She moves her hand from **A**'s *face to her throat and touches gently.*

A   I really don't know who you

B   When we go back out there I want to always be able to
see you

A   What

B   I want to be able to look at you
And see you
And know that you're mine
I don't want you out of my sight

B *increases the pressure on* **A**'s *throat.*

A Is this still
Are we
Is this part of the thing we do

B What do you think

A Because if it is I don't want to I don't like it I want to stop

B *increases the pressure on* **A**'s *throat.*

A moment when they both look really, properly scared.

B *releases* **A**.

B Course
Gosh
Yeah
Of course
It's not real

B *hugs* **A**.

A *laughs, weakly, relief.*

A I thought

B You liked it
When it makes you come like that
You like it

A Yeah
I thought
Ask me, next time, yeah?

B You fucking love it

A Yes. Yeah.

B We'd better go back in
People will be wondering where I am

18: Break

B's flat. Late at night.

A   I can't believe it – so many sold! I'm so proud of you

Pause.

B   Are you ashamed of me?

A   What did you literally listen to anything I just said

B   I thought the age gap didn't matter. But tonight – it felt like

A   Like what

B   Like you didn't want to be seen with me

A   What are you talking about

B   You always said we were the same and tonight you felt

A   What

B   Sort of – far away?
        Sorry I'm not making loads of sense

A   No. You're not

B   Do I embarrass you?

A   This conversation is ridiculous

B   Can I touch you?

A   No. No stand over there. I need you to be – if you touch me, I can't think properly

B   OK

A   You are insane. You pull me into your insane orbit and then I can't see things clearly.

B   I think it would be better, if we held each other

A   No

Pause.

B Right. Have it your way. You do realise? I saw you

A What

B I saw you. Tonight. All night. At the gallery. Tonight!
Which was supposed to be for me.
My night. For me. You were flirting.

A What are you talking about

B I could see you laughing

A This is

B You touched her arm

A I thought that wasn't real I thought that was

B Don't lie don't lie to me I fucking *SAW YOU WITH HER*

Pause.

B How do I know – that the things you do with me – you
weren't doing – secretly – tonight – with her

A You do remember I have never been with anyone else I
have never been with another woman apart from you?

B Just admit it

A I wish I could I wish I could give you the satisfaction of
being right but I can't OK I can't there's nothing there's
nothing for you to know I don't even know who you're
talking about

B Right. OK. If that's how it's going to be
You've humiliated me.

A Have you

B What. Fucking what

A I dunno. Had anything. Tonight.

B Fuck's that supposed to mean?

A Like, a drink? Or, something else?

B   How dare you ask me that?

A   Have you though

B   Of course I haven't

A   OK.

A   You fucking whore.

The buzzer goes.

B   What

They both leave. This next – we hear but don't see.

B   What the actual fuck. *How* did you get that here? They
have, like security, at the gallery!
What were you thinking?

A   I told you I didn't want it in there

B   It's not up to you. You consented to this you liked it
It's my picture
What are you doing?
LET GO

A   Ow! You're hurting me. Stop STOP

B   STOP IT NOW

A *screams.*

A   You have to stop stop stop

B   If you don't let go right now I'm going to –

The sound of **A** *destroying the picture.*

B   What are you doing you're fucking insane

A   NO

B   You're out of *control*

A terrible scream.

Glass everywhere.

Silence.

They come back. Quite a lot of blood.

A I'm I'm I'm I'm I'm

B Well.

A It's really. I think it's really [bad]

B It looks bad. I think we should go to A&E. It's OK. It's OK. It's going to be alright. I'm going to make it alright.

A Get away from me

B I promise

A Don't touch me

B I love you

A Don't

B I forgive you
It's OK.
It's going to be OK.

19: Afterwards

The grey light of pre-dawn in **B**'s *flat.*

A Thanks. Thank you.

B For what?

A For coming with me. I couldn't have done it without you. It was so loud so intense all those bright lights. You made me feel

B What

A Safe

B Good. I'm glad. Good. You are safe

A I know

B   I promised didn't I I promised I'd keep you safe

A   You did you have

B   Come here. Is it hurting?

A   Mmmmm. A bit. It's better cos they gave me those super-strong painkillers

B   I'm glad they did. They took it seriously

A   Yeah

B   It's going to be alright. I'm going to look after you

A   Thank you

B   For what?

A   For taking care of me. For taking so much care.

20: Coincidence

A public place. Busy.

B   Hey

A   Jesus holy fuck

B   What?

A *controls herself.*

A   You made me jump out of my skin

B *(laughs)*   God. Sorry. Didn't mean to. This is a coincidence!

Silence.

A/B   So / I

B *laughs.*

A   You go

B   Alright. How've you been?

A   Really?

B   What do you mean

A   Like, are you really asking me that or are you just being I don't know. Polite

B   I'm really asking of course I'm really asking

A   I've been thinking about this for weeks. I see you in the street, coming towards me.
Sometimes ten times a day. I'll see someone walking towards me and I'll think, Oh my God it's *you*, and for a moment I can't breathe. I'm so scared. And I'll feel my heart and I'll get dizzy and my eyes will swim and I'll think, What the fuck am I going to do?
What the fuck am I going to say? And when it's like my chest is going to explode – they'll get closer, the person. And I'll realise it isn't you. It's someone who doesn't even look like you. It isn't you at all

A sudden loud crack and a blinding flash of white light.

B   How've you been?

A   Fine. Fine. I'm OK.

Beat.

A   You?

B   Christ

A   What

B   Relax. I'm not going to – bite you or anything

Crack. Flash.

B   How've you been?

A   I'm OK.

B   I've missed you. I've wanted to see you. I've been thinking about you. A lot. Every day. I can't stop thinking about what we had. And I can't let it end like

this. You've crawled inside my brain and lodged there.
You've fundamentally altered the fabric of my existence.
My thoughts don't work the same way any more. Because
of you. You've made me mad. You've made me dig out
the number of my old therapist again even if I haven't
called. You've rewired me. Every time I see something
stupid and funny I get out my phone to tell you and I
can't. I find myself quietly saying your name before I fall
asleep each night

Beat.

B   Say something

Beat.

B   Say something

A   I

Crack. Flash.

B   How are you? How have you been?

A   I'm OK

B   What can we do. To make this OK?

A

B   What can I do? I'll do anything

Crack.

B   Anything

Crack.

B   Anything

A   I

Crack.

A   I'm nearly there

B   What do you mean?

A   With the consciousness thing. The proof. That it's both. A wave and a particle. That distance doesn't make any difference. That that's all we are. That all we are is intention.

Crack. Flash. This time, a tear in the fabric of reality. They both speak to the audience.

A   Sometimes I wonder if it never should have happened

B   Whenever I think about it I get excited

A   But then I think I would have ended up somewhere else

B   I feel – seared. Marked. Burned.

A   I still think about you when I wank. Every single time. Is that weird?

B   All over my body. All I can see are the imprints of you of where you were of all that's left.

A   I look at people and I wonder, what must it be like not to feel things? To feel things so much less strongly

Around them starts to gather golden light.

Golden particles. Beautiful. Incandescent. Like a cage made of light.

A   But then I think. Maybe it's better.

B   I was always doing my best

A   Which is better?

B   To feel things like this?

A   Or never feel at all?

Crack. Flash

A   Sometimes, I can feel my consciousness behaving like a particle. Colliding with things, smashing into things, breaking itself against them. But what if I let it be like a wave? It feels – too big – too much. Too much power to have. If I can change it myself – what does that mean? If my intentionality has that much impact on the world? If distance doesn't make any difference?

Observation *always* changes things. If you're watching, you're a part of it. On a fundamental level. A particulate level. A wave-like level. And everything you've ever observed stays a part of you, and you a part of it. Time doesn't matter. Distance doesn't make any difference. If you're thinking about it, somewhere, there's a little tug that connects you. Forever. All the time. All at once. Isn't that absolutely terrifying.

Crack. Flash.

The golden light vanishes.

B Hey are you sure you're OK

A Fine I'm fine I am

B It feels like it's been such a long time

A I guess it has, in a way

B How's the flat? Your flatmates. I can't remember all their names

A Fine. She's fine. You still in the same place?

B Course. They'll carry me out of there in a box

B *laughs.* **A** *doesn't.*

A You know. I picked things up with my dad
       I've asked him if he wants to start again

B That's. That's great. I'm glad. That's really great.

A Another chance, you know?

B I still think about you. Every day. And I need you to know. That I meant it, all of it.

A OK

B Please.

A   I don't know what I'm supposed to say to that

B   Nothing you don't have to say anything

A   I just – can't. Not any more. Not ever again. When I
think about us I feel.
I need to be – on my own. OK?

B *turns and walks away.*

They both stand apart for a moment. Alone.

Before.

Looking up.

A blinding flash of white light.

An impossibly loud crack.

Silence.

www.ingramcontent.com/pod-product-compliance
Lightning Source LLC
Chambersburg PA
CBHW041924090426
42741CB00020B/3469